cardboard creations

VEHICLES

Written by FIONA HAYES

Illustrated by CHRISTIANE ENGEL

Quarto is the authority on a wide range of topics.
Quarto educates, entertains and enriches the lives of
our readers—enthusiasts and lovers of hands-on living.
www.quartoknows.com

Author: Fiona Hayes
Illustrator: Cristiane Engel
Designers: Starry Dog Books Ltd and
Victoria Kimonidou
Editors: Starry Dog Books Ltd and
Ellie Brough
Editorial Director: Laura Knowles
Creative Director: Malena Stojic
Publisher: Maxime Boucknooghe

First published in 2019 by QED Publishing,
an imprint of The Quarto Group.
The Old Brewery, 6 Blundell Street,
London, N7 9BH, United Kingdom.
T +44 (0)20 7700 6700
F +44 (0)20 7700 8066
www.QuartoKnows.com

A catalogue record for this book is available from
the British Library.

ISBN 978 0 7112 4359 0

Manufactured in Shenzhen, China PP082019
9 8 7 6 5 4 3 2 1

MIX
Paper from
responsible sources
FSC® C001701
www.fsc.org

The projects in this book are for adults
to make. Children should be supervised
at all times when in reach of sharp
tools. The author and publisher accept
no liability for any injuries sustained
in making these projects, which are
undertaken entirely at your own risk.

CONTENTS

AUTHOR'S NOTE

What can you do with an old cardboard box? You can use it to make something fun to play with!

Small children love to play with an empty box. In their imagination, it quickly becomes a plane, a car or a spaceship that takes them on amazing adventures.

This book aims to inspire you, the parents or carers, to create a variety of cardboard box vehicles from easily sourced and cheap materials. You get to play with cardboard, glue and paint – hopefully with help from little hands – and your kids get to play in whatever vehicle you make. Fun all round!

All the models made for this book have been gifted to families. I've had lovely photos and some hysterical videos sent back. All have made me smile and some made me laugh out loud! It's been a delight to see the vehicles being played with and enjoyed by real children – just as yours will be!

Fiona Hayes

GETTING STARTED

Here are a few basic tips and techniques to help you get started on your cardboard creations.

WHERE TO GET BOXES

You can buy large cardboard boxes from removal companies, or look for them in your local free ads – people often give them away after moving house.

Shops will often give away cardboard boxes for free. For large boxes, try shops selling electrical goods.

Many shops put flattened cardboard boxes out for recycling and, if you ask, will be happy for you to take them away.

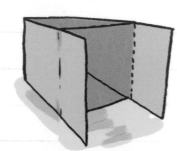

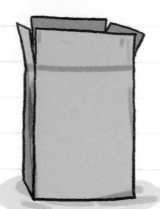

FOLDING CARDBOARD

1 To fold cardboard, start by placing a ruler where you want the fold to be. Then draw along the edge of the ruler with the end of a closed pen. Press firmly to leave a groove in the cardboard.

2 You can now fold the cardboard along the groove.

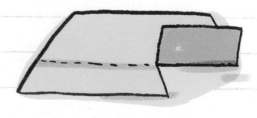

USING A CRAFT KNIFE

Most boxes will be too thick to cut with scissors. For a neat finish, it's best to use a craft knife and metal ruler. The knife is less likely to slip against a metal ruler than a plastic one.

IMPORTANT

Never allow children to use a craft knife or put their fingers near the blade.

Cut thick cardboard one layer at a time. You may need to make several cuts to get through all the layers.

To cut thick, narrow tubes into lengths, you can use a junior hacksaw or craft knife.

IMPORTANT

Never cut towards the hand that is not holding the knife.

Make sure you always cut away from your free hand.

TOP TIP

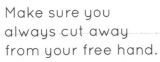

- A sharp blade will slice through cardboard without you having to press hard.
- A blunt blade is likely to slip and cause injury.

CUTTING OPENINGS WITH SCISSORS

Start by drawing the shape of your opening.

For straight-sided openings, make a hole with the end of a pen in each corner of the shape. Push the scissors into one of the holes and cut to the next hole.

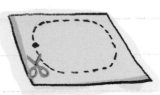

For round openings, make a hole with the end of a pen on the edge of your shape. Push the scissors into the hole and cut out your shape.

PAINTING AND DECORATING

1. Before you start painting, place a dust sheet or newspaper on the floor so you don't make a mess!

2. Make up all the separate parts of your model and lay them out. Decide what colour to paint them. It's much easier to paint the parts *before* you stick them together.

3. To paint large areas of cardboard, use emulsion tester pots (kids will need adult supervision). To get a good finish, you may need to paint each piece two or three times.

4. Adding strips of painted card to your model can give it a neat finish.

FIRE ENGINE RESCUE

Fire! Grab your helmet, check the water tank and jump aboard. Make the sound of the siren to let everyone know you're coming!

YOU WILL NEED

- 1 long cardboard box
  (or 2 boxes joined together)
- 6 wheels (see page 39)
- 1 cardboard shelf
- 2 paper cups
- 2 small cardboard circles
- corrugated card for panels,
  radiator and bumper

LADDER

- 2 cardboard tubes
- card for rungs

THE BODY

1. Start with a long box or attach two boxes together using the extending boxes tutorial on page 10.

2. Cut a door with window on both sides of the box, and a windscreen at the front – see the tutorial on page 27.

3. Add a top-hinged flap near the back of the fire engine (see page 27). This is the fire engine's equipment store.

4. Inside, add a shallow shelf for equipment, made from the base of a box the same width as the fire engine.

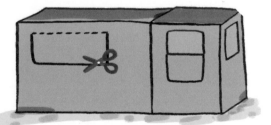

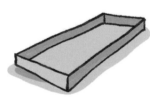

THE WHEELS

Go to page 39 to make the wheels. Glue them to the sides of your fire engine.

TO DECORATE

1. Paint your fire engine, then add some bright hazard warning stripes and discs for headlights.

2. Use painted corrugated card to make a radiator and side panel, and to cover the equipment store door.

3. Add two painted paper cup lights to the top and a bumper at the front.

THE LADDER

Make a ladder from some narrow cardboard tubes and strips of thick card. Fire engines carry their ladders on the roof.

IMPORTANT
Kids must not climb the ladder.

TOP TIP

When you glue the ladder rungs to the uprights, make sure you space them an equal distance apart.

EXTENDING BOXES

It's possible to make a box longer or taller by adding another box to it. Both boxes need to be the same width and depth.

1 On each box, cut one end up the middle and across the top and bottom to make flaps that open like a pair of doors (see page 27, step 4).

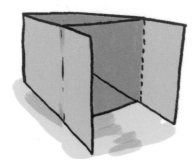

2 Slide the two boxes together so the door-like flaps on one box go inside the other box, and the flaps on the other box go outside the first box.

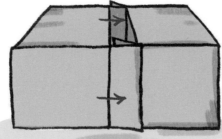

3 Glue all the flaps in place.

4 To make a box taller rather than longer, cut all the flaps off the top box and slide it over the open flaps of the bottom box.

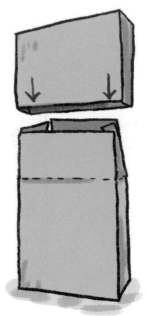

ANGLED SIDES

Some models, such as the dump truck and pirate ship, look best if you angle the sides. It's easier than it looks!

1. Open one end of the box and fold out the flaps so they stick up.

2. Draw a triangle on the box at the angle you want your object to slope.

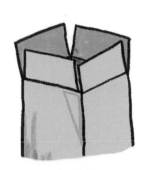

3. Cut along two sides of the triangle, leaving it hinged along the edge of the box.

4. Cut off part of the top flap shown here shaded in blue.

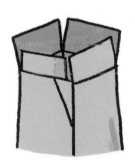

5. Cut off the pointed part of the hinged triangle so you are left with a tab that can be used for gluing.

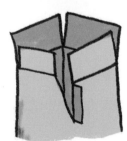

6. Repeat steps 1 to 5 on the opposite side of the box.

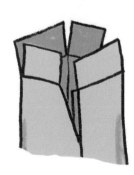

7. The box should now look like this.

8. Score a line along the front of the box level with the bottom of the two gluing tabs.

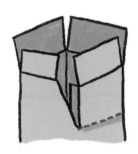

9. Fold this section in to make the sloping face of your vehicle. Secure it by gluing the two tabs to the inside of the sloping sides.

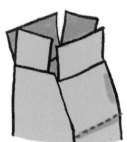

10. Score a line along the top of the sloping face (this part was originally the flap). The score line should be level with the tops of the sloping sides, as shown.

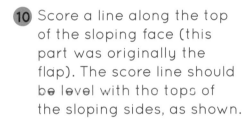

11. Fold the front flap in along the score line – the flap may need trimming to fit the new shorter top. Then fold in the side flaps and finally the back flap, which may need trimming, too. Glue the flaps in place.

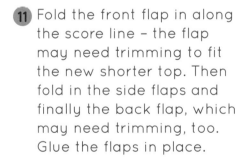

TOP TIP

It may help to lightly draw on where you want the windows to go, but you will cut these out later.

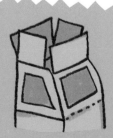

SUPER SPORTS CAR

Hop into your speedy sports car and take it for a spin in the countryside. Turn the steering wheel as you take those corners!

THE BODY

1. Cut the top section off a box, leaving a front windscreen and small side windows at one end. See page 27 for help with doors and windows.

2. Cut a door on both sides of the car body.

3. Paint the car body.

THE FRONT END

1. To make the front section, angle the end of a medium-sized box – see page 11.

2. Paint the box, then glue it to the body.

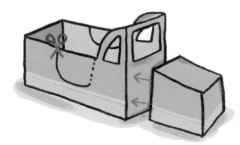

THE DASHBOARD

Glue a piece of cardboard at an angle on the inside front of the car to make the dashboard.

THE SPOILER

Add a cardboard spoiler to the back.

THE WHEELS

1. Go to page 39 to make the wheels and moving steering wheel.

2. Glue the wheels to the sides of the car and stick the steering wheel to the dashboard.

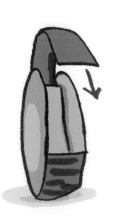

TO DECORATE

1. Add a radiator made of corrugated card, and two headlamps.

2. For a finishing touch, add door handles, a front bumper and racing stripes.

VROOOM...

TOP TIP

To support the spoiler, stick a small diamond of card underneath it.

AMBULANCE ON CALL!

Has someone been hurt? Ambulance to the rescue! Be a paramedic and help get the patient to the hospital as fast as you can.

THE BODY

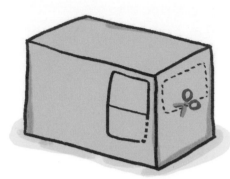

1. For instructions on doors and windows, see the tutorial on page 27. Cut a door with window on both sides of the large box, near the front.

2. Cut out a windscreen at the front end.

3. At the back end, cut two large doors.

4. Paint this part of your ambulance.

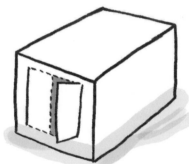

YOU WILL NEED

- 1 large cardboard box
- 1 medium-sized cardboard box, narrower than the large box
- 4 wheels (see page 39)
- 2 small card circles
- card for stripes, cross, door handles and radiator

THE FRONT END

Paint the medium-sized box, then glue it under the windscreen to make the front end.

TO DECORATE

1. Paint some hazard warning stripes on strips of card and stick them on.

2. Add two painted paper cup lights to the top.

3. Stick on a red cross, some door handles and two card circles for headlights.

THE WHEELS

1. Turn to page 39 to make the wheels.

2. Stick two wheels to the body and two wheels to the front section.

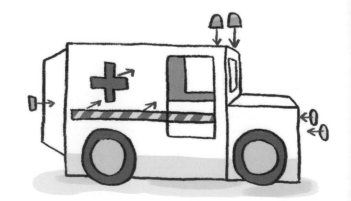

TOP TIP

To get neat diagonals on your warning stripes, stick strips of masking tape at an angle across your card and paint between the strips.

ICE CREAM FOR SALE

Do you love ice cream? Imagine creating your own special flavours and selling cones from your very own ice-cream van. Cool!

THE BODY

1. For instructions on doors and windows, go to the tutorial on page 27.

2. On one side of the large box, cut out a narrow window at one end.

3. Next to the window, cut a bottom-hinged door. This will be the serving hatch.

4. On the other side of the box, cut a door with a window for the driver.

5. Cut out the windscreen.

6. Paint the box.

YOU WILL NEED

- 1 large cardboard box
- 1 medium-sized cardboard box, slightly narrower than the large box
- 4 wheels (see page 39)
- 1 cardboard canopy
- 3 cardboard supports
- 2 small card circles
- card for stripes, radiator and ice-cream cones

THE FRONT END

Paint the medium-sized box and glue it to the front of the body.

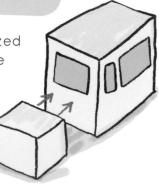

THE CANOPY

1. Make a canopy and two supports from cardboard. Paint them and stick them on as shown.

2. Stick the canopy to the supports.

THE WHEELS

1. Make four wheels using the tutorial on page 39.

2. Stick two wheels near the back and two to the front section.

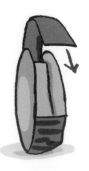

TO DECORATE

1. Paint some cardboard ice-cream cones to go on the front of the van.

2. Add a radiator, headlights and decorative stripes.

TOP TIP

Stick a folded strip of thick card directly under the hatch to support it when it's open. Paint it the same colour as the van.

ROCKET INTO SPACE

Climb aboard the rocket and 3... 2... 1... Lift-off! Watch out for rocky planets, hurtling comets and alien UFOs as you journey through space!

THE BODY

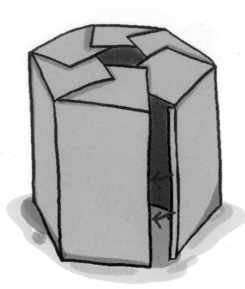

1. Make the hexagonal body of the rocket by joining together two same-sized boxes. Find out how on page 20.

2. Paint the rocket body.

YOU WILL NEED

- 2 large same-sized cardboard boxes
- 3 plastic bowls
- several large pieces of cardboard for the roof (see page 21)
- card for window frames, fins and door handles

THE WINDOWS

1. Using the doors and windows tutorial on page 27, cut out some round windows.

2. Add a door set slightly above the base.

THE ROOF

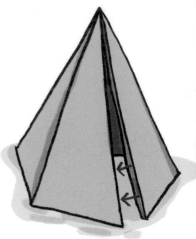

1. To make the six-sided triangular roof, turn to page 21.

2. Paint the roof, then stick it to the top of the rocket.

THE FINS

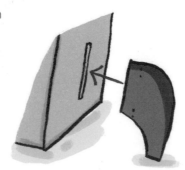

1. Cut out three fins from cardboard and paint them a bright colour.

2. Cut slits in the three sides of the rocket that have windows, and slide the fins in.

TO DECORATE

For a finishing touch, cut out and paint some card window frames and a door handle, and stick them on.

MULTIPLE-SIDED BOXES

Follow the steps to make a multi-sided rocket body. This shape would work equally well for a lighthouse, castle tower or even a summerhouse!

1 To make the six-sided rocket body, open up a tall box and flatten it out – this will give you four sides of your rocket. Take another same-size box and flatten it out. Cut off two attached sides with a long tab on each side, as shown. Join the four-fold piece to the two-fold piece by gluing one of the tabs and sticking it to the flattened box.

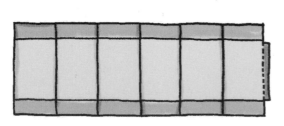

4 Fold in the top flaps. Then use your template to make sure all six corners are 120 degrees.

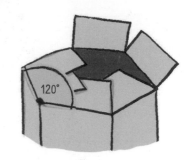

5 Glue the flaps together. Use clothes pegs to hold everything in place while the glue dries.

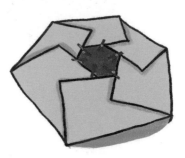

2 Fold the six-fold sheet of cardboard round to make a hexagonal box and secure it by gluing the end tab to the opposite edge.

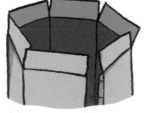

6 Repeat steps 4 and 5 at the other end of the box.

3 Draw a card template with a 120 degree corner and cut it out.

TOP TIP

You could make any number of sides. For five sides, use a 108 degree template. For eight sides, use a 135 degree template.

TRIANGULAR TOP

Use this technique to make the top of your rocket, or adapt it to make a castle turret or even a Native American teepee!

1 Cut out a card triangle to use as a template. Make the base of the triangle the same width as one side of the rocket body. The height of the triangle should be twice this length.

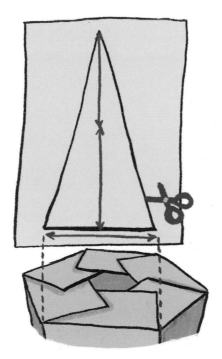

3 You need to end up with six triangles joined together, with a tab along one edge. Score along all the lines so you can fold them.

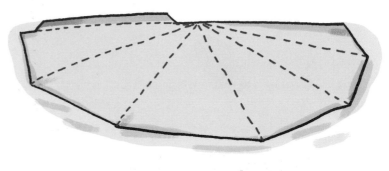

2 Use the template to draw several attached triangles, as shown. Include a tab at one end so you can join this section to the next set of triangles.

4 Fold along all the score lines to make a six-sided pyramid.

5 To secure the shape, glue the tab to the inside of the first triangle.

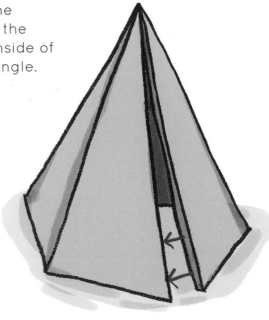

TOP TIP

If your sheet of cardboard is big enough, you may be able to draw two, three or even four triangles next to each other.

21

HOVER IN A HELICOPTER

Pretend to take off vertically, swoop low and hover above the ground in your helicopter with spinning blades. What a view!

THE BODY

1. Use the angled sides tutorial on page 11 to angle the top part of a large box.

2. Go to page 27 to make a window and entrance hole on the sides and a large window at the front.

3. Paint this section.

THE PROPELLERS

1. Turn to the propeller tutorial on page 47 to make a large propeller for the top and a small propeller for the tail.

2. Paint both propellers.

3. Cut a hole in a paper bowl and push the spindle of the large propeller through so it sticks out of the top. Glue the bowl and the base of the spindle to the top of the helicopter. Then slide on the large propeller. The bowl will help the propeller to spin more easily.

THE TAIL

1. To make the tail section, which is narrower at one end, turn to page 35.

2. Paint the tail and glue it to the back of the body.

3. Stick the small propeller to the tail.

TO DECORATE

Add some colourful stripes to your helicopter using painted strips of card.

TOP TIP

Stand the helicopter on its front when you glue on the tail.

23

LET'S GET DIGGING!

Put on your hard hat and get digging!
Have fun filling and emptying the digger's
bucket, and moving it up and down.

YOU WILL NEED

- 1 large cardboard box
- 1 smaller cardboard box
- 2 long cardboard boxes
- 6 paper bowls
- 2 pieces corrugated card
  for caterpillar tracks
- 1 piece corrugated card
  for radiator
- 2 paper cups
- 1 medium-size cardboard box
- 2 cardboard arms
- 4 cardboard discs for spindles
- 2 cardboard circles

THE BODY

1. Take a large box and angle
   the front and back of the
   top half. You can find out
   how on page 11.

2. Cut openings for the
   windows and doors –
   see page 27.

3. Attach a smaller box to the
   front under the window.

4. Paint the digger.

THE CATERPILLAR TRACKS

1. Take a long box and stick
   on three paper bowls.
   Repeat for the other track.

2. Glue some corrugated
   card, rough side facing
   out, around the boxes.

3. Paint to look like
   caterpillar tracks.

4. Attach one track to
   each side of the digger.

TO DECORATE

1. Paint some corrugated
   card and stick it to the
   front to make the radiator.

2. Add painted paper cups to
   the roof for warning lights.

THE BUCKET

To find out how to make the
bucket and attach it so that
it can move up and down,
turn to page 26.

TOP TIP

Use metallic silver paint to paint the rims of the paper bowls on the caterpillar tracks.

DIGGER BUCKET

The bucket is attached to spindles, so you can raise and lower it by hand.
Try filling it with scrunched-up paper rocks.

DIGGER BUCKET

1. Cut two discs from thick card. For safety reasons (to avoid choking hazard), these must be at least 35 mm in diameter. Stick the discs together to make a spindle and glue the spindle to one side of the digger. Repeat on the other side.

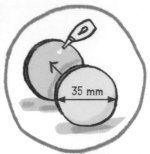

2. Make the bucket from a medium-sized box. Cut it into the shape shown here.

   Cut teeth along the top edge.

3. Cut out two cardboard arms – make them wider at one end. Cut a hole in the wide ends just big enough to fit over the spindles. Glue the narrow ends to the bucket.

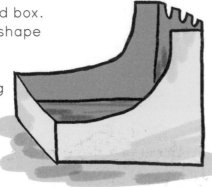

4. Slide the arms onto the spindles.

5. Glue a large circle of card over the end of each spindle to stop the arms slipping off. The bucket can now be lifted up and down.

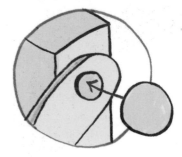

DOORS AND WINDOWS

Find out how to make doors and windows with neat edges. Once you've mastered the basic steps, you can make doors and windows for any type of model you like!

DOORS AND SQUARE WINDOWS

1 Draw your doors and windows onto the box. To get smooth, rounded corners, hold an upside-down washing-up bowl against the box and trace round it.

2 For doors and windows that open, score along the hinge with a closed pen (see Folding Cardboard on page 6). The hinge may be at the top, bottom or side. Cut along the other sides.

3 Push the door or window from the inside to open it outwards.

4 To make double doors, start by cutting down the middle, then across the top and bottom. Lastly, score the hinges.

5 For windows that are just holes, draw the window shape on your box and cut out the shape (see Cutting Openings on page 7).

ROUND WINDOWS

1 Disposable bowls make great windows. Cut the hole slightly smaller than the bowl.

2 Glue the rim of the bowl to the inside of the window hole – the bowl should stick through the front of the hole.

YOU WILL NEED

- 1 cardboard box
- 1 disposable bowl

27

DRIVE A TRACTOR

Have you ever wanted to drive a tractor? Well now you can! Climb aboard and get chugging like a noisy tractor engine.

YOU WILL NEED

- 1 tall cardboard box
- 1 same width, shorter cardboard box
- 4 wheels (see page 39)
- 1 wide cardboard tube
- corrugated card for radiator
- card for stripes and door handles

THE WHEELS

1. To make the wheels, see the wheels tutorial on page 39.

2. Make up two very large wheels to go at the back and two smaller wheels for the front.

THE CAB

1. To make the cab, angle the front of a tall box – see page 11.

2. Hold a large wheel against the side of the cab and draw round the top half.

3. Go to the tutorial on page 27 and cut out a door with window. Make sure the bottom corner is about 2 cm above the curved line. Repeat on the other side.

4. Cut out a large window at the front, then paint the cab.

THE FRONT END

Paint the shorter box and stick it to the front of the cab – this is the engine section.

THE CHIMNEY

To make the chimney, paint a wide cardboard tube and stick it to the bonnet.

TO DECORATE

Finish off by adding a radiator, door handles and some shiny stripes.

ALL ABOARD THE TRAIN

Stoke the engine, blow your whistle, wave a flag and away you go. Where will your train take you? Choo! Choo!

THE ENGINE

1. To make the cab, take a large box and stand it upright. Cut out two doors with windows and a front window – see the tutorial on page 27.

2. Paint the cab.

3. To make the boiler section, take another large box and paint it. Then stick it to the front of the cab.

THE WHEELS

1. Make up six wheels using the guide on page 39, but glue the corrugated card with the smooth side facing out.

2. Stick the wheels to the engine body.

THE BUFFERS

1. To make the buffers, cut out two card circles and stick each one to the top of a paper bowl.

2. Glue the buffers to the front of the engine.

THE FUNNEL

1. Make a funnel by sticking a paper bowl to the top of a wide cardboard tube.

2. Glue it to the boiler section.

THE CARRIAGE

1. Make a carriage with doors, windows and four wheels.

2. Add door handles to the carriage and cab.

DUMP TRUCK TIP UP

Dump trucks bump over building sites carrying heavy loads. Fill yours with scrunched-up paper stones, then tip them all out!

YOU WILL NEED

- 3 large cardboard boxes
- 6 wheels (see page 39)
- 1 cardboard hinge
- 2 paper cups
- 2 small cardboard circles
- card for the radiator, bumper and door handles

THE CAB

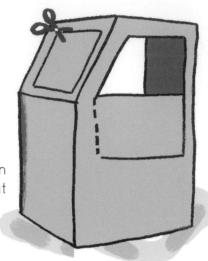

1. Using the tutorial on page 11, create an angled front to the dump truck cab.

2. Cut out a door with window on each side, and a windscreen at the front – see page 27.

3. Paint the cab.

THE TIPPER AND BASE

1. Start with two large boxes the same size. Both boxes should be the same width as the cab.

2. For the base section, shorten one of the boxes.

3. Give the other box a sloping top – this is the tipper section.

4. Cut a top-hinged door at the back of the tipper.

5. Fold a large piece of card in half. Making sure the fold or hinge is at the back end, glue the bottom of the folded card to the base and the top to the tipper.

6. Paint both sections.

THE WHEELS

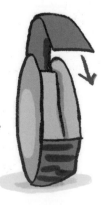

Turn to page 39 and make up six wheels. Glue two to the cab and four to the base section.

TO DECORATE

Stick two painted paper cup lights to the cab roof. Add headlights, radiator, bumper and door handles.

TOP TIP

Make a triangular wedge from a strip of thick card so you can prop the tipper up. Push it nearer to the hinge to elevate the tipper more.

TAPERING BOXES

A tapered box is narrower at one end than the other. The rowing boat, helicopter tail and submarine all use tapered boxes.

ROWING BOAT

1 Cut away the ends and one side from a long box.

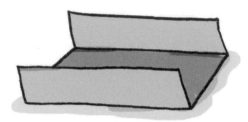

2 Flatten the box, then copy this shape on to it. Cut along the red lines and score along the dotted black lines.

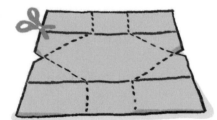

3 Fold up sections 1 to 4.

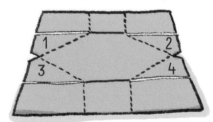

4 Now fold sections A to D up and in to follow the shape of the previous folds.

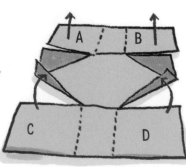

5 It should now look like this.

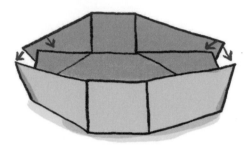

6 Glue the pointed inner flaps (1 to 4) to the outer sections (A to D).

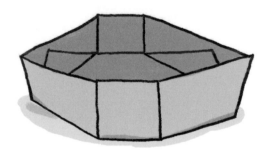

7 To make the boat stronger, fold a strip of card lengthways down the middle and stick it to the boat's pointed ends.

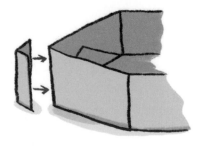

HELICOPTER TAIL

1 Copy these two shapes onto some thick cardboard. You will need to cut out two of each shape. Make sure the long sides on both pieces are the same length. Score along the black lines.

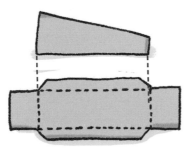

2 Glue the tabs and stick the four pieces together.

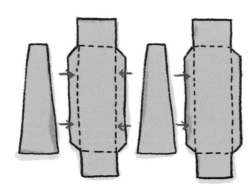

3 Fold the sides over along the score lines to make a tapered box shape. Glue the tab to the opposite edge.

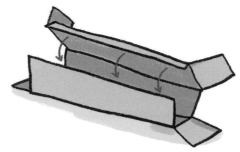

4 Fold in the flaps at each end and glue them together.

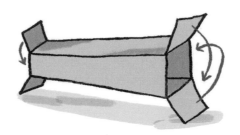

SUBMARINE

1 Open the flaps at both ends of a long box. At both corners of each flap, draw a line at a 30 degree angle, as shown. Cut along the red lines and score along the black lines.

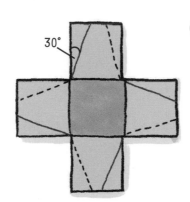

2 Fold the scored corners in. Glue each one to the inside of the next flap.

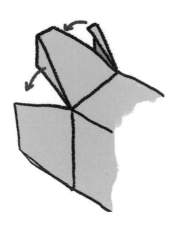

3 Once all the flaps have been glued, the end of the box should look like this.

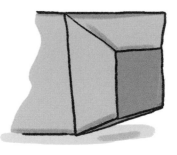

4 Cut a piece of card slightly bigger than the open end. Score along each side of the card to make four tabs. Glue the tabs to the sloping sides. Repeat at the other end.

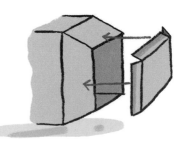

YELLOW SUBMARINE

Imagine being able to look out at all the amazing creatures in the sea. Then raise the periscope and see what's on the horizon!

YOU WILL NEED

- 1 very long cardboard box
- 1 smaller cardboard box
- 4 plastic bowls
- 1 propeller (see page 47)
- 1 periscope (see page 38)
- card to frame the windows and cover the edges

THE LONG SECTION

1. Take a very long box, and using the tapering boxes tutorial on page 35, taper both ends.

2. Go to the doors and windows tutorial on page 27 and cut out three round windows on one side.

3. On the opposite side, cut a door and another round window.

4. Paint the box.

THE INSPECTION HATCH

1. Take a smaller box and cut away the bottom.

2. Now cut away about half of the top of the box. The hole should be big enough for a small child to stand up in. Paint the box.

3. Place the smaller box midway along the top of the long box and draw round it.

4. Cut out the shape you have just drawn, keeping slightly inside the line. The hole should be slightly smaller than the base of the inspection hatch box.

5. Glue the inspection hatch box to the top of the long box so it neatly covers the hole.

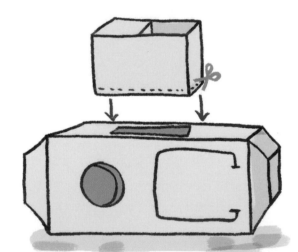

THE PERISCOPE

Go to page 38 to find out how to make and attach the periscope.

THE PROPELLER

Using the tutorial on page 47, make a propeller. Stick it to the back end of the submarine.

TOP TIP

Use strips of card
to cover the edges
for a neat finish.

PERISCOPE

A periscope allows sailors to see above the water from underwater. You can raise and lower yours, and turn it 360 degrees so you can pretend to scan the horizon.

YOU WILL NEED

- 2 cardboard tubes
- corrugated cardboard

SUBMARINE PERISCOPE

1 Take a cardboard tube and cut a 45 degree angle at one end. Glue it to the top of the other tube, as shown.

45°

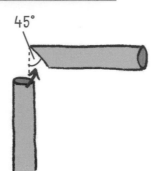

2 Stick a strip of corrugated cardboard around the middle of the upright tube. This will stop the periscope falling down into the submarine.

3 Cut two slits in the bottom of the periscope tube and slide a thick piece of card up into the slits to make the handle. Make sure the handle fits tightly so it doesn't drop out.

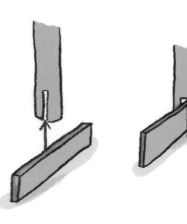

4 Cut a hole in the top of the submarine inspection hatch. Remove the handle, drop the periscope through the hole, then slide the handle back on. Your periscope can now be raised, lowered and rotated.

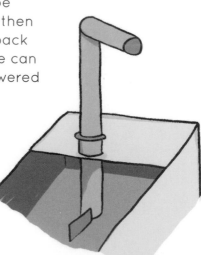

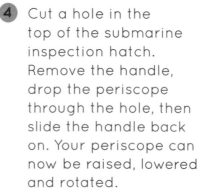

WHEELS

Once you've mastered these simple techniques, you can use them to make any type of wheeled vehicle, from a unicycle to a limousine!

YOU WILL NEED

- 2 circles of thick cardboard
- 1 paper bowl (or wide box for thicker wheels)
- corrugated cardboard strip
- card circle

VEHICLE WHEELS

1 Cut out two circles of thick cardboard. Put glue on the rim of a paper bowl, centre it rim-side down over one of the circles and stick it on. For thicker wheels, use a wide box instead of a bowl.

3 Cut a long strip of corrugated cardboard the same width as the gap between the circles. Glue the edges of the strip to the card circles. For tyres, make sure the corrugated side faces out.

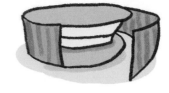

2 Centre the other cardboard circle over the base of the bowl and glue it on.

4 Paint your wheel, then stick a smaller painted circle of card in the middle for a hubcap.

STEERING WHEEL

1 Cut out a large cardboard circle for the steering wheel. In the middle, cut a hole just slightly wider than the base of a paper cup. Paint the wheel.

2 Glue the rim of the paper cup to the dashboard. If the cup base is indented, fill the indent with a card offcut. Paint the cup.

YOU WILL NEED

- 1 large cardboard circle
- 1 paper cup
- 1 small cardboard circle
- 1 cardboard offcut

3 Slide the steering wheel over the cup, then glue a card circle to the base of the cup so the wheel cannot come off. Turn the wheel!

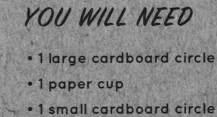

FLYING HIGH

Chocks away! Spin the propeller, then hop aboard your very own plane. Imagine all the things you might see down below!

THE BODY

1. Cut out two sides from a large box. These are your doors. Paint the box.

2. To make the round section, use the wheel tutorial on page 39, but glue the corrugated card so the smooth side faces out.

3. Paint the round section, then stick it to the front of the box.

YOU WILL NEED

• 1 large cardboard box
• 2 cardboard wings
• 2 wing supports
• 1 large tail piece
• 1 small tail piece
• 2 large circles
• 1 propeller (see page 47)

THE PROPELLER

1. Go to page 47 to make the propeller.

2. Attach it to the round section.

THE TAIL

1. Cut out two tail pieces, as shown, and slot them together.

2. Score a line on the tail piece to make a tab and glue the tab to the back of the body.

THE WINGS

1. Cut out two wings in the shape shown.

2. Fold the end of each wing down to make a tab. Glue the tabs to the sides of the plane.

woohoo...!

TOP TIP

To make the wings stronger, glue a cardboard support to the sides of the plane underneath the wings.

41

ROW YOUR BOAT

Make a rowing boat for exploring the river.
To row, sit with your back facing the front
of the boat and pull on the oars. Splash!

YOU WILL NEED

- 1 large cardboard box
- 2 narrow cardboard tubes
- 2 card ovals
- card for rowlocks

THE BOAT

1. Take a large cardboard
   box and follow the
   instructions on page 34
   to taper both ends.

2. Paint your rowing boat.

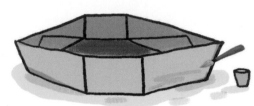

THE ROWLOCKS

1. To make the rowlocks
   that hold the oars, cut
   two pieces of card into
   the shape shown here,
   then paint them.

2. Glue the rowlocks
   opposite each other,
   half way along the
   inside of the boat.

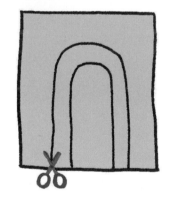

THE OARS

1. To make the oars, cut
   out two oval pieces of
   card for the blades.

2. Cut two slits in each
   blade. The piece
   of card sticking up
   between the two slits
   should be the same
   width as a narrow
   cardboard tube. Slide
   the tube into the slits.

3. Paint your oars.

TOP TIP

Make sure your oars are long enough to reach from the boat to the pretend water!

PIRATE SHIP AHOY!

Polish your hook, set the sail, hoist the anchor and sail away in search of treasure. If you see the enemy, aim and fire!

YOU WILL NEED

- 1 very large cardboard box
- 6 short cardboard tubes
- 6 straws (for the cannons)
- 1 canister (tube with bottom)
- 1 long cardboard tube
- 1 large sheet of card
- card for the flag and anchor
- string or ribbon

THE SHIP

1. To make your ship, you'll need a very big box!

2. Use the angled sides tutorial on page 11 to angle the sides on the bottom half of the box.

3. Cut out a curved section from one side to make it easier to step into the ship.

4. To make the arched windows and the top-hinged cannon doors, turn to the tutorial on page 27.

5. Paint your pirate ship.

THE CANNONS

Go to page 46 to arm your ship with cannons. If you spot the enemy, you can move the barrels to the left or right.

THE MAST, SAILS AND FLAG

1. Paint a canister and stick it to the inside of the ship, near the top edge.

2. To make the mast, paint a long cardboard tube and slide it into the canister.

3. Cut out a card sail, paint it and glue it to the mast, leaving space above it to add a flag. You can turn the sail to catch the wind!

4. Paint a big skull and crossbones flag and stick it to the top of the mast.

THE ANCHOR

Cut out a card anchor and tie on a piece of ribbon. Make a hole in the ship, thread the ribbon through and tie a knot to secure it.

For safety reasons, the ribbon must be no longer than 22 cm.

Arr!

TOP TIP

Cut out the skull and crossbones emblem from white card, or use white paint.

45

CANNONS

Heave ho, me hearties! Haul those cannons into position. If you spot the enemy, you can move the barrels to the left or right, take aim and fire!

PIRATE SHIP CANNONS

1. Paint a short cardboard tube.

YOU WILL NEED

- short cardboard tubes
- paper straws

2. Make a hole in both sides with a pencil and push a paper straw through both of the holes. Repeat for each cannon.

3. Tape the straws to the inside of the ship, so the cannon barrels poke through the doors, or gun ports. Now you can move your cannons from side to side.

PROPELLERS

Propellers drive a vehicle by moving air or water. You can make propellers for your models that actually turn - so give them a spin!

1. Cut out a single or a double blade propeller.

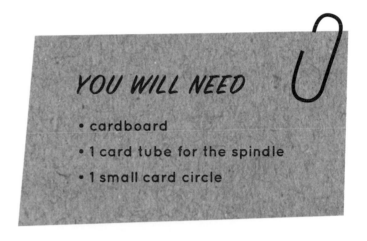

2. Use a cardboard tube for the spindle. Cut a hole in the centre of the propeller slightly larger than the end of the tube.

5. Glue a card circle to the folded-out tabs to hold the propeller in place.

3. Cut evenly spaced slits all round both ends of the tube to make tabs. At one end, fold the tabs out and glue them to the body of your vehicle.

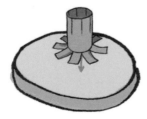

4. Slide the propeller over the tube and fold back the tabs.

INDEX